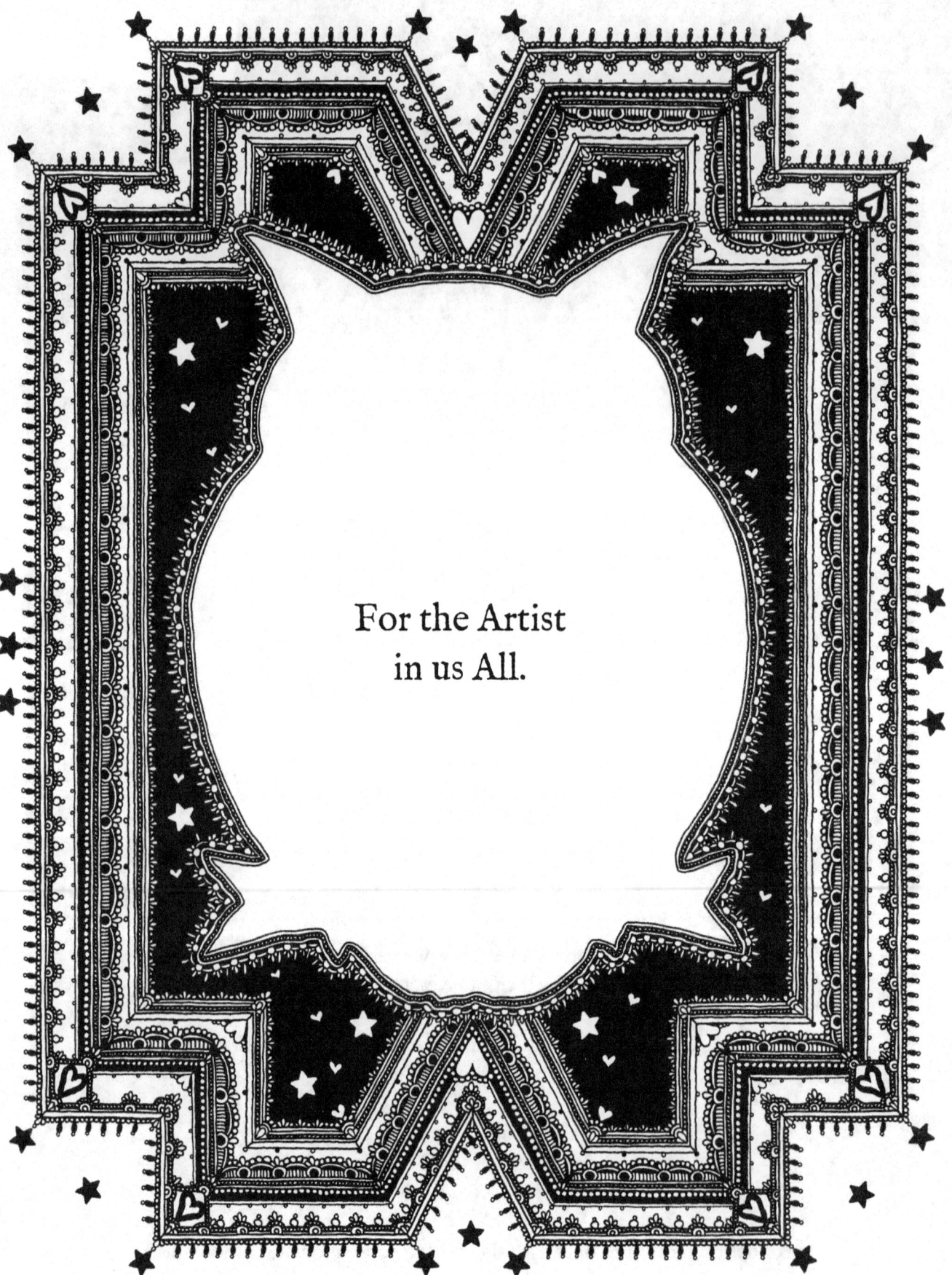

For the Artist
in us All.

Lilliam's Dream
The Coloring Book

Illustrated

by

Muriel A. Ring

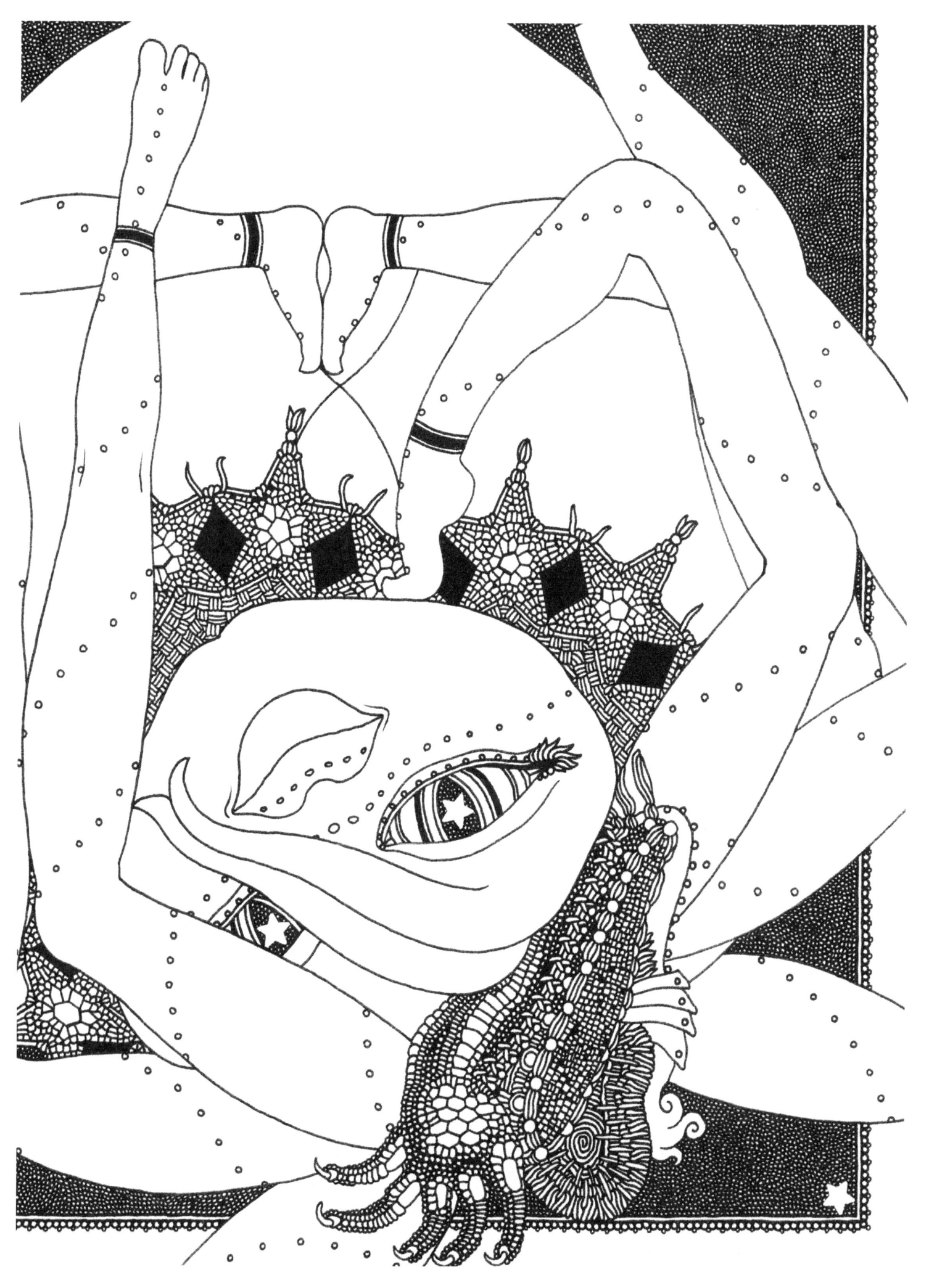

Helpful Hints...

The paper of this book accommodates
mediums such as crayon and color-pencil
very well.

Please be mindful when considering the use of
ink-pens, permanent markers, paints and watercolors.
The results could be undesirable.

Pages are not perforated, however they may be removed
with adult supervision. One method of removal
involves placing a ruler directly beneath
the area to be cut and guiding a craft-knife along the
interior crease. Properly done, this will result
in a smooth, straight edge.

Page removal is highly recommended
when choosing to proceed with
any experimental mediums.

Enjoy!